ASSURANCE

NEW EDITION

T. C. Hood

Gotham Books

30 N Gould St.
Ste. 20820, Sheridan, WY 82801
https://gothambooksinc.com/

Phone: 1 (307) 464-7800

© 2024 *T.C. Hood*. All rights reserved.

No part of this book may be reproduced, stored in a retrieval system, or transmitted by any means without the written permission of the author.

Published by Gotham Books (November 12, 2024)

ISBN: 979-8-3305-5216-0 (H)
ISBN: 979-8-3305-5214-6 (P)
ISBN: 979-8-3305-5215-3 (E)

Because of the dynamic nature of the Internet, any web addresses or links contained in this book may have changed since publication and may no longer be valid.

The views expressed in this work are solely those of the author and do not necessarily reflect the views of the publisher, and the publisher hereby disclaims any responsibility for them.

Contents

FAITH

Introduction. 5
A Slightly Christian Myth 9
The Ayers Maple 12
Passing Thoughts 13
Real 15
Lost in the Woods 17
The Quest for Identity 19
Labels, Labels, Labels. 21
Gunsmoke 22
Wax Flowers 24

HOPE

The Haircut 27
Women. 31
Appearance. 33
Purchased Kisses. 35
Dreams Before. 36
Despair. 37
When Fairy Tales are
Read to Children 38
The Cross Dresser 40
Gender Realization. 43
Gender 45

LOVE

Talking and Listening 49
The Tempo of Compassion 51
A Place? Called Home. 52

An American Family Birthday Party.......................... 55
Re-churched.. 57
And Now That I am Eighty-two 60
Smiles.. 62
Who Are You?.. 63
My Country.. 65
The Dream Makers 68
About the Author 71

Introduction

At some point in life people ask the question "Who am I?" Sometimes when very young a child will approach a parent or almost anyone a bit older and ask the question. The stories of Jesus in the Book of Matthew suggest that Jesus asked his disciples, "Who do people say that I am?"

People look into mirrors, take "selfies" with their cell phones and send them to their friends. Photographs are one way of expressing who we are. Grounded in physical appearance we see ourselves as a reflection in a mirror, in the portrait caught by a camera, in the reactions of others to us on the street. Charles Horton Cooley coined the phrase, "the Looking Glass Self." Even the person standing before the mirror recognizes that her identity is more than the reflection. But many persons agonize that the reflection is not all they would like it to be.

The poems/essays in this collection look at three areas where our identities may be challenged . Faith as opposed to doubt confronts us we determine what we believe. Hope as opposed to despair tells our attitude as we meet each new challenge. Love as opposed to hate represents our approach to relationships with other beings who are seeking assurance themselves.

*This book is dedicated to the memory of "Ginger"
(Virginia Ann Johnson)
My wife for 60 years.*

FAITH

Each New Day Brings Challenges to Faith that we understand through the lens of the point in history in which we live and move and have our being.

A Slightly Christian Myth

A curly, capped acorn fell on to the soft, moss bed of the floor of the forest. In time the Oak's leaves fell and covered it. So did the snow. As spring warmed the moist forest floor, tiny, white shoots broke through the hard brown shell. They reached up toward the sky and down into the rich, moist, warm brown earth.

The first years of the young oak were a seeking for light. Shaded by other trees, filtered through leaves, the light came very dimly to the floor of the forest. The little tree leaned first this way, then that in search of light. His leaves grew green and his stem strong in the search. His roots grew long as he searched for moisture in the earth below.

Man came to the forest cutting older trees. Storms tore branched from trees. The wind broke and tossed limbs and leaves like a giant, invisible hand. Finally, the little oak stood alone in a small clearing. With little competition for moisture and light, the young oak grew more rapidly. Still many years passed before he began to shower acorns on the surrounding grass. Through this time, the tree encountered storm, sun, drought, flood. His roots pushed ever deeper and spread more widely as his trunk grew thick with years. The piercing of his leaves by annoying insects produced a bitter gall, but each autumn the hard dead leaves fell and each spring the tender new, green leaves returned. I could tell you of the place Oak filled for the creatures of dark earth, field-forest, and sky, but that tale is too long to be told for the Oak's life entwines and embraces other lives and loses itself in their sustenance.

Man came again to the forest. Trees fell. They claimed the oak tree. He was trimmed of his magnificent branches. The stem was transported to the mill. Only the stump and small, unburnt branches remained in the field-forest, where young oaks and other saplings now begin to grow.

At the sawmill, the oak became boards large and small. The fate of this batch of lumber was to be sent to a college town. Some of the oak boards were sold to the university where it became the fine flooring of a busy seminar room. Other pieces of oak became the trimming around the doors of administrative offices. Other pieces of the oak created bookshelves in the reference room and study carrells in the university library.

A craftsman purchased the best oak boards. From this oak he made a lectern, a shelf for an encyclopedia and a rocking chair. One board was left. This board was stored in the dry area in the workshop. Next to the chestnut, walnut, maple, cherry, and other fine hard woods, the board rested quietly. Each of the pieces of furniture was finished with natural oils . The craftsman lovingly hand-rubbed the oils into each surface until an inner glow appeared not visible in the rough unfinished boards.

The lectern was purchased by the university and placed in the seminar room. The rocking chair was purchased by a professor of philosophy. The shelf was purchase by a church to house their general and religious reference books and materials. As the furniture aged with use the inner glow increased. The floor of the seminar room became scuffed by students feet and had to be refinished every few years to restore its gloss. The lectern became battered by repeated, careless jostling and occasional, thumping enthusiasms, which sent it crashing to the floor. Door frames became nicked by passing, brief collisions. Still the oak endured---lost in use.

Assurance

In the woods the slow process of growth and decay moved on. Acorns dropped by the oak, sprouted, took root and began the slow hazardous process of becoming trees. More central to our story, the stump remained with its roots spread deep and wide in the earth. During the first years, new shoots appeared as the stump tried to reclaim its lost fellowship with the sky. Failing, gradually the stump returned to the dark warm moist earth alone, for support and company. A fox made its den between the roots and beneath the stump. Tips of the roots began to die. Moss and other plants began to grow on the stump. As the years passed, bark fell off wood turned black and rotten. Water collected in the hollow of the stump, and some people came on a dark night to wash away their warts. The stump broke in pieces, gradually became the soil in which the tree-forest grows. Finally, the last pieces disappeared. After years the last fragment became a bit of organic matter in the forest-field ---lost in the eternal circle of nature's lives.

And what of the board that waits in the carpenter's workshop? And what of the rocking chair that comforts generation after generation of thinkers? Those, my children, are other tales still to be told, until they like this tale are lost in use.

The Ayers Maple

Dismal drizzle stirs the air
Quietly dampening the browning grass.
The walking heads below, bend away from the rain
Eyes fail to capture the autumn beauty caught in maple leaves.

How long has this tree inspired
Musing professors, bored students
Looking up and gazing out—Only to turn again
To work refreshed on top of this broad hill.

Twenty, thirty, forty years
Of leaves green, red and bright yellow
Against the stark black branches
Have marked the last curtain call of summer.
I wonder and notice again
A small stone plaque placed to remind
Succeeding generations that those who were once young
Loved maples, too, And oaks
 enough to plant them.

Colors fade. Leaves fall.
Thoughts cloud, words fail.
Only trees remain, embracing the earth
 and sheltering those who love them.

Passing Thoughts

She stopped me to ask
  If I didn't find the illness of three friends
Appearing in one small group
  Something to fear or to produce wonder.

Like finding two four-leaf clovers in a small lawn ...
A lucky draw in poker—some chancy happening...
Like winning the lottery or breaking a mirror in one hundred pieces.

What do you say to a person who has been told that their life will end?
It certainly isn't s new thought.
When you reach that stage of life after retirement, the names in the obituary columns are not strangers any more
---but acquaintances, people you've met, friends, and friends of friends and sometimes a spouse or son or daughter..

What do you say to a friend that is beginning to pass?
"Eat! Drink! Be merry for tomorrow you may die!"
"You have fought the good fight! You have lived well!
We shall remember your triumphs and be glad!"
Silence. A firm handshake. A tearful hug. A tight-lipped smile. A muffled sob.
"Keep a stiff upper lip!"
"Do not go quietly into that good night!"

Relationships are the stuff that make men and women.
We represent relationships in such strange ways, particularly in the public eye.
Like the President's lady removing a wedding band from her finger
Placing it on the finger of her dead husband's body as she left the coffin for the last time.
Sending flowers to a family we have never graced with such a gift in life or
Money given in memory for some positive program in a dependable institution.

The body is such a fragile thing to hold the good and bad attributed to the person.
So when a body is buried, cremated, rotted, scattered ---completely out of sight-
Memories and material productions remain.

Songs, poems and buildings
  Photographs and paintings,
    Children, inventions, books,
Good deeds mixed with bad ones
  Symphonies and recordings,
Gardens, fruit trees, forests.

YOU are a part of me! And even when both of us are gone---
    Thoughts, memories, ideas, visions linger!
Only God knows where!

Real

Keeping it "real
You have to know
The reference point
Where your journey began.

You have to know
Where you should go
To reach your promised land

Many voices may contend
To guide you
On your way
But be assured
Please be steadfast
Do not be led astray.

Guiding lights are everywhere.
Choices are made each day
To walk, to run to carry on
To work, to rest, to play
To read,, to talk, to just discuss
To take another's hand to
Steer by stars
To scan a map
In any foreign land.

When you are lost
You need to stop
To clear your clouded mind
To quiet fears
To ponder doubts
To let them go
To move on with your find…

Hang on to REAL
Just keep the frame
And you will be assured
That walking in the way with God
Will always be preferred.

Lost in the Woods

Walking through the woods
Among the trees, the ferns, the untrimmed bushes
Plants of all shapes and sizes growing wild.
Not my neighborhood with well-mowed lawns
Planned and tended flowers
Color-filled beds, that break-up the swaths of green
Grass that doesn't require paint to make it fresh and bright.

When you walk in the woods
You can forget
Man-made piles of brick
Of stone, of steel .
You brush against some leaves
And feel the moisture of the world
You start to know that plants have feelings too.
The vines, the ferns, wildflowers are alive.
Look over there a cluster of mushrooms growing
In that shaded spot.
What is that stirring in the bush?
Hopping from branch to branch
A tiny bird
Not some gaudy, colorful, feathered friend
Just a little grey and white nuthatch.
If I had not seen the movement
I'd have missed
The presence of another creature
Not made still
By roots planted in the earth.

No! Like a little bird I can
Wander among the trees so tall
Struggle through bushes too thick to make a path
If I am not careful

To mark the way I came
I may not know
How to return to places
I have been.

Lost in the woods
Gives one time to ponder
What it means to be rooted in the earth
To have to wait for the world
To come to me to bring
Some songs of merriment and mirth
Or maybe to bring fire
Destroying the quiet glens of peace
Or clearing just enough, create a path
That passes through my lostness…

Lostness
Lostness
Tremble at the word
What can being mean
Not rooted in one place
In order just to live..

So many of us are just uprooted
And now we wander
Trying to find our place
Outside the quiet of the forest floor.

Lost in the world of brick and steel
Of churches, schools, factories and stores

Where can we plant our roots?

The Quest for Identity

Americans, They like to feel
That THEY are quite unique.
The unusual hat they wear
A t-shirt line
The shoes upon their feet.

The hair-cut style that they chose
Perhaps the color hair
 Curly or straight
Blonde, black or red
Some shade of brown
They care

I know a woman who loves hats
She wears them just to church
I know a man who likes ball caps
He wears them just to work.

Does everybody like to tell
A story with their clothes
Some businesses are seen to thrive
On topical t-shirt lines

If there's a protest going on
We let our chests proclaim
That we believe in humankind
We won't forget the Maine.

An incident from long ago
Could have been a t-shirt theme.
Now some new cause to champion
May become our latest dream.

To advertise…to advocate
To wear upon our breast
To show that we support the cause
To claim it with our dress

Labels, Labels, Labels

The world is full of labels.
That everyone creates
Convenient ways to tell us
What we should love OR hate.

It might be just a can of corn
Prepared to be salt-free,
A piece of "wild-caught" salmon steak
Or apples grown organically.

The grocery store is full of them.
The pharmacy is too.
If we could stop the labels there.
The world would be less "blue."

But all my friends and enemies
Don't stop with marking food
They go outside each shopping place
Sometimes they are quite rude.
Labelling people they tell me
Who I should love or hate.
That's not our job, for we cannot
Know every person's fate.

Gunsmoke

She grew up watching cowboys and cowgirls.
Roy Rogers and Dale Evans
And hearing cowboys sing
Like Gene Autry and the "Sons of the Pioneers."
Songs like "Cool Water" and "Tumblin' Tumbleweed."
"Oh! Bury me not on the Lone Prairie!"

On Saturday at a local movie show
She could see a part of a serial western.
You could tell who the bad guys were.
They wore the black hats.
The good guys wore white hats--
They won the gun battles,
And they put an end to the plots of the bad guys.
Saturday afternoon theater was a place apart
"Close by" a "home away from home."
A world with its own clear rules--
While the bad guys had their moments
In the end the good guys won.

Only later did that popular drama set
In the American West
"Gunsmoke" appear.
Television made the character, Matt Dillon,
Marshall of Dodge City, Kansas famous.
She loved to watch him and his deputies
First Chester and later Festus
Help bring a bit of order to a frontier

Assurance

To make community for Kitty and Doc
In a frontier town where…
The fastest gun and the strongest fist fighter
Often seemed to prevail in ending the chaos.
But always Matt came through in the end.
He stood for law and order
Against self-seeking pride of place.

She was older now.
The children she had raised were gone.
The demands of daily job had ceased.
Household tasks were being handled by her husband.
Craft projects were laid aside.
The computer screen was dark
Jigsaw puzzles were becoming more difficult to complete.
The ability to remember was going away.
Finding word books were laid aside.
But she still knew when the gun smoke cleared.
That good had prevailed.

And it was still OK to have a good night's rest.
To sleep in peace…Someone was in charge.

Wax Flowers

Wax flowers
  Petals perfect bloom eternally
Forming an archetype
  Among less perfect blossoms born of nature.

Wax flowers
  Melt; wilting in the heat
Heat that formed, molded them
  Between softly pressing fingers
That held the promise of distortion or perfection.

Wax flowers,
  A craftsman's impression
Created to promote unnatural passions
  Once removed from glimpsed reality
Which gave them birth.

HOPE

Hope comes from encounters and from our struggle at realizing a vision or finding a purpose/cause to purse.

ASSURANCE

The Haircut

Haircuts give a kind of hope
The barber's view of yourself.
Or maybe a way to reaffirm
That you are still just you.

When you settle in the chair
The stylist soon will ask
Do you want a cut or trim?
To assess the task.

Will you have your hair short or long
To reach down to your waist,
To make pigtails or just a bun
A French twist to your taste?

Skinhead, mohawk, crew -cut, you say
Pixie cut, a mass of curls
A combed look like a duck tail.
Pageboy with bangs
Might be the look that would you satisfy
Or just a trim with careful layers
Could avoid a stifled cry.

Perhaps you thought that the gray
Was not yet "right for you"
Or that long hair you "loved to brush"!
Was daily trouble too.

You thought perhaps a bit of dye
Might just restore
your fading grasp on youth
A permanent to add some curl
Would bring fresh look to birth

When sitting in the stylist's chair
Whether she's young or old
You hope her vision of your head
Is something bright and bold.

For some long hair grown to sell
Which doesn't offer risk
Just might provide a bit of cash
To purchase a lover's gift.

The barbershop has an essential tool
You find on every wall
Mirrors provide so many views
No one can see them all.

So nowadays when caps can shade
To bring your skin relief
If you have chosen to be bald
You travel without grief .

Unless you're going to a game
You won't paint your head
But if blue hair or even green
Might be OK he said

Your stylist often likes to talk
She knows that only you will hear.
After all she can whisper
Some gossip in your ear.

Assurance

You better select a barber
Who shares your worldly views
Otherwise, you may receive
Opinions you would not choose.

Home permanents like *"Toni's"*
Produced a persistent stink.
Even after thorough washing
Your hair out in the sink.

In a corner of the shop/salon
Where nails and toes were cleaned
The odor there was acetone
When all the painting is done

Along with hair dressing
Comes a cloud of smells
Think of old bay rum hair tonics
Once popular with males.

I liked the smell of sandalwood
The feel of talc dusted on my neck
With horsehair brush that tickled
Just before the barber
Gave the drape a final snap.
And said, " I think you're finished.'
Then I got up from the chair
To see to check the different look
From what I'd brought before
I was seated there.

Perhaps I'd go to ask a friend
To see what they saw now
If I had changed my image more
And messed it up somehow.

How did you choose your barber?
Recommendation from a friend?
Reputation of a brand?
The location of the shop?

Was your trip to the barber
Alone or with a friend
Sometimes you choose this adventure with
A companion on whom you depend
To give an "honest opinion"
On what your new appearance provokes.
When you walk down the street
Will passersby think your new look is a joke?
Or are you now the beauty queen
Or a handsome man
An ardent team supporter
Not just another fan.
Whether you meant to say the word
Your haircut says it all.
That is the hope for everyone who answers to the call.

Women

What does the capacity to bear a child
Mean in the construction of one's identity?
And when a woman gives herself
To a man and becomes pregnant

What is the nature of that gift
During the nine months of carrying new life
 Then the nature of the gift emerges .

So now there is a baby..
..the arrival whether natural or induced
…was not without effort or pain.

And someone to assist
..someone to catch the infant
..perhaps a midwife or a doctor
Circumstances may require the father,
..transport driver, even a bystander could be called.

Complications ?
 Babies do not always arrive on schedule
..or at the woman's home, or hospital bed
..or delivery room
And surgical intervention may be necessary.
Childbirth is the natural end
..to pregnancy
..and yet prenatal care
..may reveal possible complications .

And when birth is accomplished
..and when a healthy babe and mother
..are pronounced
The woman and the parent can simply rest
...enjoy the new-born life
That She has nourished for nine months
...and those who have supported and observed
..can gently sigh
      expressing some relief.

The Bond formed at conception
...has matured.

The healthy baby sleeping
..quietly inspires a renewed confidence
..that humankind may even have a future.

Appearance

The quest for an identity
Americans like to feel
That they are quite unique
The hat they wear
The t-shirt line
The shoes upon their feet.

The haircut style
That they choose
Perhaps the color hair
Curly or straight
Blonde, black or red
Some shade of brown
They care.

I know a woman sho loves hats.
She wears them just to church.
I know a man who likes ball caps.
He wears them just to work.

Does every body like to tell
A story with their clothes
I know a busines seems to thrive
On topical t-shirts.

If some protest is going on
We let our chests proclaim.
That we believe in humankind.
We won't forget the Maine.
An incident from long ago
Could have been a t-shirt theme
Now some new cause to champion
May become our latest dream.

To advertise! To advocate!
To wear upon our breast
To show that we support the cause
To claim it with our dress.

Purchased Kisses

Your soft, warm lips touch mine
With studied, cool tenderness,
The passion that once caused us
  To hug so bear-like lost in the warm fuzziness of a younger love
    Has evaporated
In the desert of our bedroom.

I ask permission to kiss you now
Lest my too anxious embrace
  May cause you pain
And I wonder at the slow response of your lips to mine..

The kissing booth at the school bazaar
Swims into my memory
Sweet young women offer kisses for $2.
The booth stands among tables offering home-baked cookies,
Pies, layer cakes, second-hand clothes, and craft being sold
To raise funds for some good cause.

Kissing is a good cause.
Like music, a kiss is a most intimate moment.
Freely given a kiss says a mouthful—
Better than a thousand words of poetry .
A child's kiss is full of innocence.
A baby's kiss is full of trust.
A spouse's kiss recalls the joys of the years.
A lover's kiss tries to say more than can be captured in a touch.

What have we paid for the kisses we have given—
To each other, to our friends, to the world?
Each casual kiss may cheapen or grace our display of affection.
Does your kiss have a price?
Kisses are much better when they are freely given .
Let the little ones come for they point the way to heaven.

Dreams Before....

Silent is my bedroom
in the black.
Below the misted memories
Rise fogging consciousness.

Alone—Beyond

Unworldly comprehension.

Dreams before sleep
are best
Forgotten quickly.

Despair

Hard-breathing or
Calm-caught
Conventional I
Stand where?

Who cares?

Unfelt God's love
Or the indiscriminate sunlight
Or the cold wind that froze my nose.

Complacent in despair,
Repair.
My argument scarred.
I find
My fading flare
Falling into night.

When Fairy Tales are Read to Children

My Grandma Hood read them to me.
I learned about the woodcutter, the wolf, the grandmother
   And little Red Riding Hood
I learned about the shoemaker and the elves that saved his business
Hansel and Gretel and the wicked witch with the gingerbread house
Of course, the little mermaid and the match girl
Some tales were sad with tragic endings
The Brothers Grimm and Hans Christian Andersen
But most were short and could be read and thought about
   In an afternoon on the way home from school.

And before
   I helped Grandpa with the milking.
In those days we only kept two cows---no milking parlor, no milking machines
   Just a stool and a bucket to fill with sweet tasting warm milk
   I squeezed each of the four teats until each of the udder's quarters was empty.

Then back to the farmhouse where Grandma was in her rocking chair.

If you had been to the barnyard on Grandpa Hood's farm you knew about
　　Sheep, goats and rats. You didn't have to imagine the delight of the people
　　In Hamlin when the pied piper lured the rats out of the village. And you could easily
　　Imagine the power of the charge of the Billy-Goat Guff
　　Butting the troll off the bridge and into the river.

Then when Mom or Dad came by ---It was time to go home.

The tradition of reading fairy tales to children somehow got passed on
　　And we read to our children, The Hobbit, The Lord of the Rings -trilogy,
　　The Narnia Chronicles
And when our children were grown we read all the Harry Potter tales to each other.

The Cross Dresser

Clothes are one way
You try to say
Just who you think you are.
You snap a photo with your phone
To twitter near -or far,
Perhaps you post a word or two
And wait for some respond
The web allows for many views
Right now or in days beyond.

Some like to paint their faces
To shape with arch their brow
With careful shading contour
The facial shape to cover any shadow
To minimize that too large nose
Create a pouty lip
Attempt new facial beauty
That passes close exam.
A mirror says, "You did it!"
A post says, Yes, you can!"

To frame that face
With just right hair
Requires a new wig
What length is right
Should there be bangs
Human hair is not required,
What is the proper length and cut?
A girlish image to acquire.

Assurance

Now you can turn
To body shape
You need for proper dress
Fill out the space above the waist
With two protruding breasts.
Next cinch that belly
Pad those hips
The hour-glass recall
The dresses will fit better
The mirror tells it all.

Before you try to slip your legs
Into some silken hose
You tuck those male parts
In your crotch
Inside a dancer's gaff.
No need to raise some questions
About illusions truth.

The nylon hose slip up your legs
A garter belt holds them high.
They lead down to some high-heeled shoes
A well-designed stiletto pump
With toes that just peek through .

Perhaps you choose a shirt-waist dress
Or pencil skirt and blouse
Something casual for your stroll
On an afternoon outside the house.

Complete the look
With matching purse to carry
On your walk inside a nearby shopping mall
To demonstrate that while you're out
You won't provoke some staring looks or talk.

If you're not too nervous,
Head up now--
Lined eyes open wide.
A pleasant smile on your red lips
You've practiced walking in those heels;
Don't stumble or collide!
You hear them click on pavement.
Your fears will soon subside.

You may not be a beauty
Or look like someone whose clothes are worn.
And all the people who pass you by
Will neither smirk nor frown.

Perhaps you stop to check some dress
You chat with a store clerk
You thought that they would just object
Not so! Each sale is a perk.

Your adventure ends quite well.
You'll live another day.
Now you can feel a touch of pride,
For you have had your say.

Gender Realization

When little boys began to play and want to wear a dress
When little girls like to rough-house and get dirty in the mud
When adult observers intervene and start to change the play
When no one cares what little one wears, we need not stop to say
To question what's appropriate in gesture, talk or clothes.
Each culture has established views "That Everybody Knows!"

When the babe came from the womb, the doctors made the choice
Anatomy determined sex. The infant had no voice.
Nor did the parents except with anatomy anomaly
Even then choices offered avoid ambiguity.

But choices made when humans are so very small
May not reflect the options that will begin to call.
When children play, games do not depend on gender role or style
Who runs fast, who does not hurt, who has fun all the while.

Dress up may provide a chance to wear, to find how fabric feels
While boys may find silk panties or a pair of nylon hose
And girls try denim overalls and heavy woolen socks
The link between gender and clothes is established early on Boys
may want to try the look their moms wear each day While girls
may identify with dads when they dress up to play.

Face painting may create a look defined as beauty
Face painting for the hunt or war may be for camouflage
Gender differences appear along with facial hair
A bushy mustache and a beard define a manly face
Females should confine the hair to well plucked eyebrows
And a clean space above the lip. Eyelashes should be well-defined.
The skillful make-up artist can create a look to minimize the nose
Can contour and shade a face to feature the most attractive bone
Perhaps the cheek, perhaps the chin and even the forehead's dome.

As our person grows older they make a choice of where to put their
Allegiance to a male or female look currently in style
Within their culture's corner of the gender world.

But what about those who refuse
To choose a gender role.
What about those who call themselves "gender fluid"
What is that? What do nonbinary or transgender mean?

As folks grow older the choices made become
Less determining and they find room to overcome
A simple shy reluctance to don a dress or suit.
Girls may be boys; boys may be girls
And that is all there's to it.

Benedict reported on the *berdache* man/woman in American plains Indian tribes.
These individuals realized their dual gender in ways not part of our traditions.

So where are we today among the butch and sissies
as we walk down the street?
Undecided still confused by people that we meet.
The convinced nudist offers another plan
Let's just discard our clothing and frolic in warm sand.

Gender

On that morning
She awoke and said
I am not a tree
When she saw Adam standing by
She said I am not a he.

We start to claim
Who we are by
Looking all about
At first we don't know much at all
We'd just like to find out.

To understand the difference
To label what we see
We find it easy to understand
That we are not a tree.

And yet as living beings
We start to walk around
To find ourselves
We start to smell
Begin by hearing sounds
We start to feel the good damp earth
Moist between our toes
To see the soft pink petals
The scent and fragrance of a rose.

So when and how do we come
To recognize that she is not a he
And he is not a she....
Is this something we must learn
Or is it just to be.

We put great stock in using props
To tell each other how we feel
We cloth our naked bodies
We paint our skin
We add to and shape our form
Or wear a mask
Some message to convey
About just how we feel inside
   Do we feel like a girl?
   Do we feel like a boy?
How should we show
  just how we feel .

I guess we have to learn
    some lessons
we must choose
what we love
what we spurn
That concludes the "news."

LOVE

C. S. Lewis wrote a book about four loves described by the Greeks. Love may not explain everything, but it helps.

ASSURANCE

Talking and Listening

Communication between two people happens
When one person listens
   with all their faculties
And the person speaks
   with all their moving parts.

Attention to what another person says
   With all their words and actions
Is the beginning of good listening .

Sometimes when two people are
 In each other's presence
They talk to each other but stop listening.
When that happens, communication stops.

Person one clearly remembers what was said
To person two
And THEY are right --- they said it !

Person two remembers what was said to person one
And they are right --- they said it.

The problem is that person one wasn't listening
And the problem was person two wasn't listening.

So Person One and Person Two exchanged
Words and gestures
But communication wasn't happening.

When two people stop listening to each other
They can have long expressive exchanges of words and gestures
In writing by text, in recordings by tape, even face-to -face in the same room.
BUT when the listening stops
The Relationship Ends.

Why do you want to listen to another person?
The other person may have information that you need
To complete a task
To understand what is happening around you
To make your relationship with that person more meaningful

Some people say that the reason you listen to another person
Is to show them that you care about them.

Some people say that listening to another person is the beginning of love for that person.

My belief is that listening is the beginning of friendship
And friendship is the beginning of love .
Because communication is difficult
If you listen to another person fully and carefully
Until you have heard and understood fully what the other person said
That makes a partnership enduring and worthwhile.

Don't stop listening.
Don't stop talking
Just understand communication doesn't happen
By exchanging words.
Love begins with the desire to know, to understand, to care.

The Tempo of Compassion

Silent beauty of rhododendron blossoms
Startles me to reflect.
Bright pink and red colors bloom
then perish as the petals fall .

What can a man
If he does not see
Recognize life fade !

The brightness dims washed out
by the sunshine. Flowers wither and fall.

A human knows
And is moved.

Compassion thrives among
Those who pause to see
the beauty of flowers.
Those who are too busy
Sometimes forget the tempo of mercy.

A Place? Called Home

Many –perhaps, all of us
..have a card file of sayings in our heads
Or somewhere we store words
..that make us more than
Flesh, blood, sinew, bone.

Home is what you make it.
Home is where the heart is.
Home is not a place.
You know you are home when
..you arrive to loving arms.

Home is the first page on your web-site
Home is the top of your Facebook posts
Home is your starting point
..when you travel
And home is where you
…when you return.

A familiar song says
 "Happy the home
When God is there,
   ..Where love fills every breast.

May be "love" is our home
May be "faith" is our home
May be "hope" is our home.

Assurance

Home is where you are from
...when you are away.
Home is what awaits you
  ...when you return.
Sometimes home is
   ...where you put all your treasures—
   ...even if it is just a beaten-up grocery cart.

Sometimes when you are at a place
   ...where all your treasures are gone
   ...and you are homeless without a place called home.

Even the solitary hermit
Seeks shelter from weather
...rain, snow, wind, sun's powerful rays..
Not to mention the exhausting, prying eyes and ears
   ...of human contact

Of course, home is what you make it.
A frayed, canvas tent
..staked in an isolated spot
A carboard box
  ..in an out of the way alley.
But permanent or temporary
...just Now it is home
Because you say it is!

How does a child come to feel a place
  ...comfortable enough to nest
  ...to call their home.
Well, maybe Edgar Guest was right
  ..when he said
"It takes a heap o' livin' to make a house a home."

One thing is surely true
Home is not a place found on a map
Nor does it have a permanent physical address.
Home is a state of mind
  ...and just like other places in the mind
You cannot comprehend its beauty
  ..or take its measure
Except with the inner eye (we sometimes call the heart).

So! Stop!
Where you are
Pause
Behold the beauty
That you see around and
Feel that you are home!

Even NOW.

An American Family Birthday Party

Last night we had a party
For a woman—eighty-two.
A sister-in-law, three sisters:
Two couples; four singles, too.
A farmer's friend, a son,
A daughter growing wild.
Four wedded and two widowed,
One away and one who smiled.

The meal was mashed potatoes
Gravy on the side
With steak cooked in the oven
Green beans from garden wide,
The salad ---just leaf lettuce
Pickles from the store,
Tea and milk and coffee.
Sliced bread made days before.

We all sang "Happy Birthday,"
When choc'late cake was served,
Red Jell-O, whipped cream topping.
Desserts to dull the nerve.
Recipes were shared once more-
A source of compliments;
So, with our guts stuffed full enough
Our hostess was content.

Last night, we had a party.
The ritual it, was sweet.
With hugs and kisses all around,
Our fellowship complete. ...

While other bodies starving
a half a world away woke
hungering for garbage!
Oh! Lord! Am I the way?

Re-churched

The voice of prophecy echoes
in the empty sanctuary-
Empty because it is no longer
A safe refuge from the crisis
Of an insanely split world.

Stoppered ears –refuse to listen
to the cracking, bursting explosive
Message of the gospel.
Covered eyes refuse to see
The shambles surrounding
Antiseptic churches---trying to be beauty spots
Within the slums of decaying cities

No longer are church pews
the cushioned comfortable place for
Sunday morning dozing .

The sanctuary that was the church
must explode---like some
critical mass of love
creating joy---
shattering, flinging fragments and splinters of broken crosses
and chunks of crumbled altars out...
Raining debris
on a waiting community
forcefully driving the remnants of sacred symbols
deep into fainting hearts of
an all too secular world.

Then as the splinters of God's love
Thaw the frozen hearts of the people who
Have tried to remain cool in a world
That refuses to recognize the need for repentance and even
Revolution in our treatment of people, places and problems
By allowing the blanket of God's love comfort and redeem us.

If She Could Speak

When I'm with you
Then I know who I am.
You make me glad
That I am still alive.

But when you go
You know that I feel lost.
You are not there.
And I no longer know
Just who the hell I am.

You know how much I love you
For we have loved
These many- many years.
And if you go
Well, I just –just don't know
Who I shall be.
Can you just understand?
Can you feel doubt
The feelings of confusion
Rise in me.

Just stay with me
Hold closely to affirm
Just say the words
That make me
Who I am.

And Now That I am Eighty-two

When I was twenty-two
When I was thirty -three
When I was forty, fifty, sixty-five
Some people stopped to make something of my age.

But now that I am eighty-two
No one really cares to comment much
Or even take note except to say, "You just don't look that old!"

Yes I do remember collecting scrap iron and metal during WW II
Yes I remember when that war ended.

Following the dropping of an atomic bomb on two cities in Japan.
With the recognition that some limits might have to be placed on how much destruction should / could be permitted without destroying the ability of the earth to sustain human existence.

But wars continued
And Americans have fought and died in warfare
Mostly around the world ---usually at least one ocean away.
But oceans don't separate me from the rest of the world's people
Like they did when I was less that ten years old.
Geographical distance just isn't what it used to be....
Communication is almost as quick as a lightening bolt.
So, information that I can use tomorrow can be compiled in India tonight
And be on my desk in the morning ready for presentation..

Assurance

I have more books at my elbow and whole libraries at my fingertips
Through the digital world of electronically organized and stored technical reports, stories, numbers and maps---information enough to lose your very sense of where you are and perhaps even when you are
...NOT TO MENTION WHO???

So now that I am eighty-two what does it mean to count birthdays.......
Careers and friends have passed through my life and yet my consciousness remains
Perhaps it is a gift from God, as some would say.
Or not...

Smiles

Her mother used to tell her
"You are not fully dressed until
   You put on your smile.!"
And I think that she believed her.

In sixty years of marriage
We had many happy days
But there were days of sadness too
Days when we mourned friend's death
   Or some unexpected tragedy
And days when we bowed in prayer for friends who'd fallen ill.

So Ginger often smiled and
   Those who met her smiled back
Just like the old song told
The smile made folks happy and
Helping hands grew bold.

Then one day she came to feel
Lipstick enhanced her smile
A shade of red—a little pink
You could see the smile for a mile.

When we see a smiling face
Our mood may change to glad
The clothing may be shabby
Not in the best repair.
The setting may be cluttered
   Waiting for someone to care….
But if we see a smiling face ----
Our mood changes to glad..

ASSURANCE

Who Are You?

Who are you?
Are you nobody too?
Those used to be light-hearted questions
A way to start the day
To chase away the fleeting thought,
"I don't know what to say!"

But now they are a cry for help.
I do not always know
If you are someone I should know
A trusted friend or foe.

You might be an old lover.
You seem a gentle friend,
But then again, I am not sure.
I just cannot depend
On waking up to who I am!

About that! Can you?
It is very confusing.
I don't know what to do.

You know that it is really hard
To discard- perhaps a faded letter
   A photo someone took
   A book that once I treasured
A pressed flower so long dead
A tattered newspaper clipping
   When a couple was wed.

Of course, I don't remember
   The event, the date, the place.
Only that these meant something
That gave me grace to know.

Mementos just are pieces
Of life strewn here and there
Gathered into boxes
(stacked away upstairs
   in attics or in basements)
Sometimes with not much care.

But now I ask the question
   With serious intent
Who are you?
Are you nobody too!
Don't throw me in the garbage
   Or the recycle bin.
Just help me to remember

Then I can just be me again.

My Country

My land of liberty
Is built on cooperation
Not coercion.

My freedom comes
From the joy of working together
Not self-promotion.

Friendship begins
Racism ends through
Acceptance not rejection
Of difference.

Building a future together
Starts with a plan
The plan begins with a dream
The dreamers saw a vision
Where people lived together
Respecting, helping one another
To live free of want
To live in health
To grow in strength
To show that vision
To the world (democracy)

We no longer communicate
Through the limits of smoke signals.
First the telegraph
Then the telephone
Now the internet and the cell.
New technology produced the means
To share our thoughts and dreams
Around the world in images and texts.

When I was young who could have imagined
The party line replaced by sharing contents of a book.
Unpublished research reports, pictures of an injury
A painting actually---not simply drawn in words
But shown in colors pixels capture that human eyes can perceive
Transmitted through the internet around the world or
Even into space beyond the limits of gravity.

My land of liberty
Is filled with wonders.
The promise of this world
Sustains my hope in a bright future
Where all beings live in peace
Where human wars have ceased
Where mutual-aid and understanding do prevail
And finally, at last, we understand
The universal languages of love.

Another voice cries out…
"This is a utopian delusion..
The jaded cynic cries out
"Please be serious!
History says you're wrong!
It cannot be!"

Too many of this country's children starving.
Pandemics still arise and kill at will.
Cooperation even within a single nation
   Struggle to survive.
How can you even dream a world,
Where nations share their wealth with each other
In the name of love?

Assurance

Perhaps that latest newscast has left
You slightly deranged;
Perhaps you brain has suffered injury
When you fell down and
Hit your head upon that large stone put in your way.

How can you expect us to endorse the triumph of love,
When there is so much hate
When there is so much greed
When people joy in suffering
More than in sharing
When leaders use power to accumulate, to hoard
Rather than share the wealth they have achieved.

The vision of a sharing world is false
Just like liberty ---only a fleeting dream
Justice fades as differences prevail and
Once more neighbors say
"if you are not like me then go away
Or if you must stay bow down to me and serve my wants."

In My Country the question still echoes
Across the years from 1776 until today,

"Can we have justice, liberty and freedom for all?
Will love or hate prevail?
America!
Is it only a dream?

The Dream Makers

I was born in the home of dream makers.
They fed me on the strength and flexibility of self-giving love.
They nutured me on the discipline of tasks that required response
   but were not beyond my abilities.
My bearers opened our home to my friends so that they felt
   the fellowship that we shared.

My Father gave me ideas out of his imagination and taught me,
   by example, that farmers do write poetry.

My Mother showed me that even the simplest household chores can be done
   with pride in perfection of achievement.

The family taught me that doing tasks together for the benefit of others is
   one of God's greatest gifts.

My Father took me to the mysterious presence in a quiet woodlot and
   showed me the glowing beauty of a ripe peach at sunset.

My Mother gave me the scents and tastes of the kitchen and the quiet strength
   found in listening well before speaking.

Prayers were our daily litany of thanksgiving and renewal.

My home had books, a time to talk.
My home had visits to the old who were seeing visions.
My home had music as we practiced piano lessons.
My home had visitors from here and there---always with ideas to share
    over a slice of pie, a glass of milk or some other pleasant offering.

Our home was a haven ---a treasure trove of resources where I could dream
    In bedroom, hayloft, orchard or attic.
A place where I could count on help from the family to find the best we had
    To bring dreams to reality.

I have read about parents who have killed their children's dreams

Our parents helped us
    Always from the beginning
    As they continued to do for others
    To live in a world where
    Today's dreams become tomorrow's accomplishments.

About the author

T. C. Hood, Ph.D., Professor Emeritus of Sociology, University of Tennessee, Knoxville received his university education at Michigan State and Duke. The Bachelor of Arts degree with high honors was awarded at M.S.U in June 1960. In August. 1960 "Ginger" Johnson married "Tom." She provided family support by teaching during his first years in graduate school in addition to his graduate research assistantship. Duke awarded the A.M. degree in sociology in 1964 and in August of that year, their son, Christopher Charles, was born. Ginger had by this time begun teaching at Meredith College in Raleigh, NC. In September 1965, Hood began teaching at the University of Tennessee, Knoxville. Their daughter, Heather Kay was born in September 1969 not long after Duke granted Hood the Ph.D. degree in Sociology. During those years Ginger provided great family support and much assistance in typing drafts of the dissertation.

Professor Hood has taught courses primarily in collective behavior and social movements, research methods, social psychology, environmental sociology and American studies. In addition to teaching at all undergraduate levels and graduate levels, he had directed and served on more than 100 masters and doctoral committees. He served as Executive Officer of the Society for the Study of Social Problems for nineteen years.

A committed Christian, Hood is a life-long member of the United Methodist Church having served on local, district and annual conference committees. He and Ginger have been active 4-H leaders in Knox County for more than 40 years. He has received the College of Arts and Sciences and National Alumni Association Awards for Public Service.